grade 3

D1479935

For full details of exam requirements, please refer to the current syllabus in conjunction with *Examination Information & Regulations* and the guide for candidates, teachers and parents, *These Music Exams*. These three documents are available online at www.abrsm.org, as well as free of charge from music retailers, from ABRSM local representatives or from the Services Department, The Associated Board of the Royal Schools of Music, 24 Portland Place, London W1B 1LU, United Kingdom.

CONTENTS

In this album, editorial additions to the texts are given in small print, within square brackets, or – in the case of slurs and ties – in the form ⌐. Metronome marks, breath marks (retained here where they appear in the source edition) and ornament realizations (suggested for exam purposes) are for guidance only; they are not comprehensive or obligatory.

Footnotes: Anthony Burton

DO NOT PHOTOCOPY © MUSIC

Alternative pieces for this grade

Music origination by Barnes Music Engraving Ltd
Cover by Økvik Design
Printed in England by Halstan & Co. Ltd, Amersham, Bucks.

Tyrolean Air

from *Ten National Airs with Variations*, Op. 107 No. 5

Edited by
Ian Denley

BEETHOVEN

Among the minor works of the great German composer Ludwig van Beethoven (1770–1827) are 16 sets of *National Airs with Variations* for flute or violin and piano, which he composed in 1818 and 1819 for the Edinburgh publisher George Thomson. This is the theme of one set, a tune from the Austrian Tyrol called 'A Madel, ja a Madel', complete with a suggestion of yodelling. The pause in b. 21 is an invitation to the flautist to add a short improvised lead-back to the new phrase (although this is not an exam requirement).

Andante alla Siciliana

Second movement from Flute Concerto No. 6

A:2

Arranged by
Sally Adams and Nigel Morley

MERCADANTE

Like most Italian composers of his time, Saverio Mercadante (1795–1870) wrote mainly operas – more than 60 of them, in fact. But he first established his reputation, while still a student at the Naples Conservatory, as a composer of concertos. Six of them were for the flute, an instrument he studied at the Conservatory, and the last of these, written in 1817, was his first work to be published. This is an adaptation of its central slow movement, in the lilting dance rhythm of the siciliana. According to the conventions of the time, the reprise of the first strain, from b. 29, could have some added ornamentation (although this is not an exam requirement).

Allegro

Fourth movement from Sonata No. 3 in F, Second Suite

Continuo realization by
Willy Hess

PEPUSCH

Johann Christoph Pepusch (1667–1752) was a native of Berlin, but from about 1700 he was active in London as a string and keyboard player, director, teacher, researcher into early music, and composer. He is probably best known for arranging the popular tunes in *The Beggar's Opera*, the smash hit of the theatre season in 1728. His compositions include two sets of six 'Solos for the Flute', sonatas originally for recorder, accompanied by a keyboard and/or a bass instrument. This is the finale of the third sonata from the second set, published around 1709. The dynamics are suggestions for exam purposes and may be varied.

High School Dixie

from Dancing Flute

B:1

HEINZ BOTH

Heinz Both (b. 1924) is a German composer and arranger who specializes in jazz styles. 'High School Dixie' comes from a collection of ten pieces, each linked to a different part of the world: its title refers to American secondary schools and the idiom of Dixieland or traditional jazz.

B:2

Seashore

No. 19 from *The Microjazz Flute Collection 1*

CHRISTOPHER NORTON

Born in New Zealand in 1953, Christopher Norton went to study composition at the University of York in 1977 and has since settled in England. His extensive *Microjazz* series features progressive pieces in popular styles for various instruments. In 'Seashore', the quavers should be played evenly, with the piano part suggesting the gentle lapping of waves.

Hurdy-Gurdy

from *Dances of the Dolls*

B:3

Arranged by
Ian Denley

SHOSTAKOVICH

The Russian Dmitry Shostakovich (1906–75) was one of the leading composers of the 20th century; his works include operas, ballets, 15 symphonies, 15 string quartets, and a good deal of music for his own instrument, the piano. His seven *Dances of the Dolls* of 1952–62 are simple piano arrangements of movements from his ballet scores; this piece, originally from his 1935 ballet *The Bright Stream*, is further arranged here for flute and piano. A 'hurdy-gurdy' is an instrument on which a melody is played on a keyboard acting on a string, over a drone produced by the turning of a wheel – though here, rather than a drone, there is a constantly repeated alternation of two 'oom-pah' chords.

Plaintive Flute

No. 21 from *Fifty for Flute*, Book 1

ALAN BULLARD

Alan Bullard (b. 1947) studied with Herbert Howells at the Royal College of Music. As a composer, he has written in most genres both for amateurs and for professionals, although he is perhaps best known for his choral and educational music. To achieve its effect – *malinconico* in the tempo marking means 'melancholy' – this little piece needs careful attention to dynamics and tone colour.

Mélodie polonaise

from *L'art du phraser*

C:2

Edited by
Edward Blakeman

DEMERSSEMAN

Mélodie polonaise Polish Melody; **L'art du phraser** The Art of Phrasing

Jules Demersseman (1833–66) was a Dutch flute virtuoso who studied in Paris and spent most of his short life there – though he never gained a teaching appointment at the Paris Conservatoire because of his opposition to the new Boehm-system flute. He composed many pieces for his instrument. This 'Polish Melody' is in the dance rhythm of the polonaise but in a song-like style.

Flowing

No. 8 from *More Easy Jazz Singles for Flute*

RUSSELL STOKES

Russell Stokes (b. 1958, London) is a flautist, pianist, teacher and composer with a particular interest in jazz styles. His *Jazz Singles* series introduces students to technical challenges within a melodic and contemporary idiom. He says about this number that 'the tongue should not be used too firmly, but should have an almost lazy feel'. Notice the contrasts of dynamics between **f** and **p**, accentuated by the bluesy B♭s at the beginning of the **p** phrases.